Tastes&Flavors
of **HAWAI'I**

Tastes&Flavors
of HAWAI'I

MUTUAL PUBLISHING

Library of Congress Cataloging-in-Publication Data

Tastes & flavors of Hawaii.
    p. cm. -- (Little Hawaiian cookbooks)
Summary: "A collection of the best and most favorite flavors and tastes of Hawaii's unique local dishes"--Provided by publisher.
    ISBN 1-56647-778-6 (hardcover : alk. paper)
    1. Hawaiian cookery. I. Title: Tastes and flavors of Hawaii. II. Series.
    TX724.5.H3T38 2006
    641.59969--dc22

                                        2006010748

ISBN-10: 1-56647-778-6
ISBN-13: 978-1-56647-778-9

Compiled and Edited by Muriel Miura
Design by Emily Lee
Photos on page 5, page 7, page 18, page 22, page 26, page 70, page 74, page 76, and page 78, by Ray Wong
All other photos © Douglas Peebles

First Printing, May 2006
1 2 3 4 5 6 7 8 9

Mutual Publishing, LLC
1215 Center Street, Suite 210
Honolulu, Hawai'i 96816
Ph: 808-732-1709 / Fax: 808-734-4094
E-mail: mutual@mutualpublishing.com
www.mutualpublishing.com

Printed in Korea

Table of Contents

Hawai'i's white-sand beaches, sun and surf, and fragrant blossoms lure an endless stream of visitors to its shores today, but over a hundred years ago, peoples of various ethnicities flocked to Hawai'i for different reasons. They traveled great distances from far corners of the world, bringing with them the intent of working hard and the hope of earning a good living. They also brought their foods and culture, which, over the years, melded into its own unique cosmopolitan mix of cuisine and customs from all over the globe. Significant cultural influences that comprise Hawai'i's "local" culture today come from Polynesians, Chinese, Japanese, Portuguese, Koreans, Filipinos, Puerto Ricans, and most recently, Southeast Asians such as the Vietnamese, Thai, Laotians, and Cambodians.

Hawai'i is also a place where rice is the staple starch, although rice was never eaten by the native Hawaiians whose staple was poi. The mixing of different foods in a meal started during the old plantation days when lunches were taken in boxes and shared. Today's classic plate lunch, with its two scoops of rice with macaroni salad, is built around an entrée of meats such as kalbi kui, sweet sour pork, or macadamia crusted mahimahi, but the choices are endless depending on where one goes to eat.

The Hawai'i Regional Cuisine movement, whose roots arguably can be traced to the rudimentary kitchens of the old plantation days, has changed the way we look at Hawai'i's foods. The addition of fresh fish dishes or mesclun mixtures of fresh Island greens suits the lifestyle of Islanders who are interested in "healthy" living. Some dishes such as Kona Crab Puffs have a gourmet flair while Pūlehu Short Ribs, Aku Poke, Char Siu Bao, Cascaron, and Almond Tofu sound exotic but are simple to prepare. This new wave of eating well and healthy with a touch of fancy is indicative of a vibrant, changing Island lifestyle.

The collection of recipes selected here represents a sampling of Hawai'i's many flavors. No matter which recipe seems the most appealing, there is something to suit every taste. The meals created from this cookbook are certain to evoke warm memories of Hawai'i for years to come.

Mai e 'ai (come and eat)!

PŪPŪ/
APPETIZERS

Easy Char Siu Bao

Serves 10–12

Char Siu Bao is Cantonese for roasted sweet pork-filled buns.

1 can (10.2 ounces) refrigerated Parkerhouse rolls or biscuits

Filling:
1 cup char siu (roasted sweet pork), chopped
2 tablespoons minced green onion
1/2 teaspoon soy sauce
Dash of white pepper

2 tablespoons salad oil

Combine Filling ingredients and mix thoroughly. Place one tablespoon filling in center of each circle of dough; pinch edges of dough together to seal. Brush tops of dough with salad oil. Steam in waxed paper lined steamer for 15 to 20 minutes.

Tip: Bao may be baked instead of steamed. Follow package directions for baking.

Yakitori (Teriyaki Chicken Kabobs)

Makes about 18 kabobs

1 pound boned chicken, cut into bite-size pieces
1 can water chestnuts, drained
1 bell pepper, seeded and cut into 1-inch pieces

Marinade:
1/4 cup soy sauce
3 tablespoons sugar
1/4 cup mirin (sweet rice wine) or sherry

Bamboo skewers, soaked in water 45 minutes

Thread chicken, water chestnut and bell pepper alternately on skewers. Combine Marinade ingredients; marinate kabobs 10-15 minutes. Broil, basting frequently with marinade as it cooks; about 4-5 minutes on each side. Serve hot.

Tip: Cook kabobs on outdoor grill.

Kona Crab Puffs

Makes about 3 dozen

1/2 cup water
Dash salt
2 tablespoons butter or margarine
5 drops hot liquid pepper sauce
1/2 cup flour
2 eggs
1 tablespoon chopped chives
3/4 cup Kona crab meat, drained and flaked

Salad oil for deep-frying
1 carton (6 ounces) purchased guacamole dip

In a saucepan, combine water, salt, butter, and hot pepper sauce. Bring to a rolling boil over high heat; add flour all at once, remove from heat, and stir vigorously until mixture is smooth and leaves the sides of the pan. Add eggs, one at a time, beating well after each addition or until dough is smooth and satiny. Stir in chives and crab. Drop dough by teaspoonfuls into oil heated to 375°F. Cook, turning occasionally, until golden on all sides, about 2 to 3 minutes. Drain on absorbent paper. Serve with guacamole dip.

Aku (Tuna) Poke

Serves 6–8

1 pound raw fresh aku (tuna) fillet
1 tablespoon sesame oil
1 teaspoon toasted sesame seeds
1/4 cup minced green onion
1 Hawaiian red chili pepper, seeded and minced
Salt to taste

Cut aku into 1-inch cubes; combine with remaining ingredients and toss lightly to blend. Refrigerate and chill well before serving.

Variations:
• Substitute aku with 'ahi, hamachi, sea bass, or other fish commonly used for sashimi.
• Season raw fish with 2 tablespoons soy sauce, 1 tablespoon sesame oil, 1/2 teaspoon red pepper flakes, and 2 tablespoons minced green onion.

Hawaiian Party Mix

Makes about 4 quarts

6 cups bite-sized shredded wheat cereal
6 cups O-shaped puffed oat cereal
6 cups bite-sized shredded rice cereal
1 box (7-1/2 ounces) very thin pretzel sticks
1 can (6-1/2 ounces) macadamia nuts
1 cup butter or margarine
1/2 teaspoon onion salt
1/2 teaspoon celery salt
1/2 teaspoon garlic salt
1 tablespoon Worcestershire sauce
10 drops liquid hot sauce

Combine cereals, pretzels, and nuts in a large baking pan. In a small saucepan, melt butter or margarine; stir in remaining ingredients and let stand 2 to 3 minutes. Pour butter mixture over cereals and mix lightly to coat. Bake at 250°F, 1 to 2 hours, stirring well every 20 to 25 minutes. Cool and store in an airtight container.

Salted Soybeans

Serves 5–6

6 cups soybeans in pods
2-1/2 quarts water
2 tablespoons Hawaiian (rock) salt

In a large saucepan combine soybeans, water, and salt; cover and bring to a boil. Reduce heat and simmer for 8 to 10 minutes or until beans are cooked but still crunchy; drain and cool. Serve as appetizer.

Note: Use Hawaiian salt sparingly in dishes as it tends to make foods saltier than ordinary table salt.

Cream Cheese-Chutney Spread

Serves 10–12

1 package (8 ounces) cream cheese
1 cup mango chutney
2 tablespoons crisp bacon bits

Crackers of choice

Place cream cheese on serving dish or cheese board. Spoon chutney over cheese and top with bacon bits. Serve with crisp crackers.

Variation: For something different, grind a clove of garlic and a handful of cilantro leaves in a mini food processor; stir in a few tablespoons of mayonnaise and a dash of hot sauce to make a Garlicky Green Mayonnaise. This is a great spread for a tomato or grilled chicken sandwich.

Curried Mayo-Yogurt Dip

Makes 1-1/2 cups

1 cup mayonnaise
1/2 cup yogurt
1 tablespoon Worcestershire sauce
1–2 tablespoons curry powder
1 tablespoon powdered mustard
1 teaspoon salt
1/4 teaspoon white pepper

Place all ingredients in a blender or food processor and blend thoroughly. Chill and serve with crudités, bread sticks, or crackers.

Variation: Stir up a refreshing yogurt sauce with chopped cilantro, minced onion, salt and a dash of freshly ground black pepper. Serve with grilled vegetables or tossed greens.

SALADS & DRESSINGS

Liliko'i (Passion Fruit) Dressing

Makes about 1–1/2 cups

1 can (6 ounces) frozen passion fruit juice, thawed
3/4 cup salad oil
1 clove garlic
1 teaspoon paprika
1/2 teaspoon salt
1/2 teaspoon celery seed

Combine all ingredients in blender; cover and blend well.
Serve over fresh fruit salad, chunks, or slices.

Green Papaya Salad (Som Tam)

Serves 4–6

2–3 fresh red chili peppers, seeded and minced
2 cloves garlic, minced
1 green papaya (about 3 cups), peeled and shredded
1 tomato, sliced into strips
2 tablespoons nam pla (fish sauce)
2 tablespoons lime juice
Lettuce leaves

Garnishes:
Lime wedges
Red chili peppers, optional
Chopped peanuts
Fresh cilantro or basil leaves

Grind garlic and chili peppers together using mortar and pestle. Combine papaya, tomato, nam pla, and lime juice; add garlic mixture and toss lightly. Place papaya salad on lettuce leaves and garnish with lime wedges, chili peppers, peanuts and cilantro or basil to serve.

Variation: Substitute shredded carrots or cucumber for the green papaya.

Creamy Tropic Salad Dressing

Makes about 2 cups

1/3 cup mayonnaise
1/3 cup salad oil
1 tablespoon tarragon vinegar
1 cup catsup
1/2 teaspoon dry mustard
2 tablespoons sugar
1 tablespoon honey
1-1/4 teaspoons salt
1 teaspoon Worcestershire sauce
1 teaspoon lemon juice
1 teaspoon steak sauce
1 clove garlic, crushed
Dash of pepper

Place mayonnaise in mixing bowl; slowly beat in salad oil. In a separate bowl combine remaining ingredients and blend into mayonnaise mixture.

Tropical Ambrosia

Serves 6

3 oranges
3 bananas, sliced
1 cup pineapple cubes
1 cup freshly grated coconut
Fruit juice of choice, optional

Peel and remove white membrane from orange sections. In a large bowl, combine all fruits and gently toss together with grated coconut. If desired, add fruit juice. Chill 2 to 3 hours before serving.

Variations: Vary fruit combinations as desired, or add marshmallows, maraschino cherries, and/or nuts.

Macaroni-Potato Salad

Serves 10–12

1/2 pound elbow macaroni
8 hard-cooked eggs, shelled and wedged
3 red potatoes, cooked and cubed
1 package (10 ounces) frozen peas and carrots,
    thawed and cooked
1 tablespoon salt
1/2 teaspoon white pepper
2 cups mayonnaise

Cook macaroni according to package directions; drain well; cool. In a large bowl, combine macaroni with eggs and potatoes. Sprinkle salt and pepper over; toss gently and cover with plastic wrap. Chill overnight.

Add mayonnaise to chilled macaroni mixture; mix gently to combine. Adjust salt, pepper, and mayonnaise as desired. Serve cold.

Chinese Chicken Salad

Serves 4–6

1 medium head Romaine lettuce
1 small head iceberg lettuce
1/4 cup chopped Chinese parsley
1/2 cup chopped green onion
1/2 pound char siu, slivered
1 cup cooked chicken, slivered
1 cup won ton chips
1 tablespoon toasted sesame seeds

Sesame Dressing:
1/4 cup sesame oil
2 tablespoons rice vinegar
1/2 teaspoon salt
2 tablespoons sugar

Wash lettuce; drain thoroughly and tear into bite-size pieces. Add parsley and green onion; toss lightly and chill well. Before serving, arrange char siu, chicken, and won ton chips over greens, then sprinkle with sesame seeds. Combine Sesame Dressing ingredients; mix well and pour over salad greens to serve.

Kim Chee (Korean Style-Pickled Cabbage)

Makes about 1 quart

2 pounds won bok (celery or napa cabbage)
1/2 cup Hawaiian (rock) salt
1 quart water

Seasonings:
2 teaspoons minced Hawaiian red chili pepper
1/4 teaspoon minced garlic
1/2 teaspoon minced fresh ginger root
1/2 teaspoon paprika
1 tablespoon sugar

Wash cabbage and cut into 1-1/2-inch lengths. Dissolve salt in water and soak cabbage in brine 3 to 4 hours. Rinse and drain. Combine Seasonings and add to cabbage, mixing thoroughly. Pack into 1-quart jar; cover loosely and let stand at room temperature 1 to 2 days. Chill before serving.

Tofu Salad

Serves 6–8

1 block firm tofu, drained and cubed
1 can (16 ounces) salmon, drained and flaked
1 large tomato, diced
1 small onion, chopped
1 package (12 ounces) bean sprouts, washed and drained
1 bunch watercress, cut into 1-1/2-inch lengths
1/2 cup chopped green onion

Dressing:
1/2 cup canola oil
1 clove garlic, pressed
1/4 cup soy sauce

Layer ingredients on large platter in the following order: tofu, salmon, tomato, onion, bean sprouts, watercress, and 1/4 cup green onion.

To prepare Dressing, combine oil and garlic in small saucepan; bring to a boil. Remove from heat; add soy sauce and remaining green onion; mix well and pour over layered ingredients. Serve immediately.

MAIN DISHES

Tofu Meatloaf

1 block firm tofu, drained
2 pounds lean ground beef or poultry
1 package (1-3/8 ounces) onion soup mix
2 eggs, slightly beaten
1/4 cup minced green pepper
1/2 cup dry bread crumbs
1/2 teaspoon salt
2 tablespoons brown sugar
1/4 cup soy sauce
1 teaspoon prepared mustard

In a large bowl, mix tofu, meat, soup mix, eggs, green pepper, bread crumbs, and salt. Pour into 9-inch round pan; press lightly and bake at 350°F for 30 minutes. In saucepan, combine sugar, soy sauce, and mustard; cook over low heat until sugar dissolves and pour over loaf. Bake additional 15 minutes or until done.

1-1/2 pounds thinly sliced pork cutlets
1 teaspoon salt
1 cup panko or fine dry bread crumbs
1/2 cup flour
2 eggs, beaten
Vegetable oil for frying

Sauce:
1/3 cup Worcestershire sauce
3 teaspoons catsup
1 teaspoon sugar
1 teaspoon soy sauce
Dash of hot liquid pepper sauce

Pound pork cutlets, then sprinkle with salt. Dredge cutlets in flour, dip in eggs, then coat with bread crumbs. Deep-fry in oil heated to 375°F until golden brown. Drain on absorbent paper. Combine Sauce ingredients; mix well and serve over hot cutlets.

Fried Rice

Serves 6–8

2 tablespoons salad oil
1/2 pound char siu, slivered
1 teaspoon shrimp sauce, optional
1/2 cup chopped green onion
1/4 cup chopped Chinese parsley (cilantro or coriander)
6 cups cold cooked rice
2 eggs, beaten

Seasonings:
1 tablespoon soy sauce
1 tablespoon oyster-flavored sauce
1/2 teaspoon salt

Heat oil in wok or skillet. Stir-fry char siu with shrimp sauce, green onion, and Chinese parsley for 1 minute; add rice and seasonings; stir-fry additional minute. Add egg; mix and toss gently 1 minute or until egg is cooked. Serve hot.

1 pound fish (mahimahi, sea bass, snapper, cod) fillet, cubed
2 cups water
2 cups diced potatoes
3 slices bacon, chopped
1 onion, chopped
2 cups milk
Salt, pepper, and butter to taste

Minced parsley
Crackers

Place fish in saucepan with water; bring to a boil then lower heat and simmer and cook until fish flakes easily when poked with a fork, about 10 minutes. Remove fish, reserving stock, then flake. Add potatoes to stock and cook until tender but firm, about 10 minutes.

Meanwhile, in a skillet, stir-fry bacon with onion until translucent. Add bacon, onion, fish, and milk to potatoes. Season with salt, pepper, and butter to taste. Garnish with minced parsley and serve with crackers.

Easy Sushi Rice (Vinegar-Flavored Rice)

Makes 4 cups

1-1/2 cups short grain rice
1/4 cup sugar
1/4 teaspoon salt
3 tablespoons mirin
6 tablespoons rice vinegar
1 cup water

Rinse and drain rice. Combine remaining ingredients in a saucepan, stirring well to dissolve sugar and salt. Add rice. Cover and bring to a boil on high heat; reduce heat to low and continue cooking until rice is tender, about 20 minutes. Turn heat off and steam 5 additional minutes. Using rice paddle, fluff rice and cool completely before making sushi of your choice.

If using an automatic rice cooker, just combine all ingredients in rice pot and follow manufacturer's instructions for cooking.

8 shrimp
1 cup water
1/4 cup rice vinegar
1 tablespoon sugar
1/2 teaspoon salt

4 cups Sushi Rice (see page 35)
1 teaspoon wasabi paste
8 slices fresh raw fish ('ahi, sea bass, hamachi, salmon)
8 slices cooked octopus, optional
Soy sauce

Shell, clean, and butterfly shrimp. Put shrimp and water in a saucepan; bring to a boil; drain. Combine vinegar, sugar, and salt; mix well. Add shrimp to mixture and marinate 2 hours.

Place about 2 tablespoons Sushi Rice in right hand and lightly press into a thumb-shaped mound, about 2 × 1 × 1-inch in size, forming and smoothing rice with the index and middle fingers of the left hand. Dab a pinch of wasabi paste on mound of rice and top with a shrimp or slice of raw fish. Repeat process topping each sushi with shrimp, fish, or octopus. Serve with soy sauce in individual dishes.

Marinade:
1/2 cup soy sauce
2 tablespoons salad oil
2 tablespoons sugar
1 teaspoon minced fresh ginger root
1 clove garlic, crushed

2 pounds top sirloin steak, cut into 1-inch cubes
18 mushrooms
18 cherry tomatoes
1 can (8-1/4 ounces) pineapple chunks, drained
1 green pepper, cubed

Combine Marinade ingredients in a large mixing bowl; stir until well blended. Marinate meat for 30 to 60 minutes. Thread meat, mushrooms, tomatoes, pineapple, and green pepper alternately on skewers and place on broiler pan rack to cook. Broil about 3 inches from heat for 8 to 10 minutes; turn and baste with Marinade. Broil additional 8 to 10 minutes or until to desired doneness.

Tips:
• Soak bamboo skewers in water for 1 hour before using to prevent burning.
• Combine Marinade ingredients in zip-top plastic bag; marinate beef in bag and toss bag for easy clean-up.

1 pound medium shrimp (15–20)
1 pound fish fillet, cut in 2-inch strips
Flour
Salad oil for deep-frying

Batter:
1 cup flour
1 cup cornstarch
1 egg, slightly beaten
1 cup ice cold water

Tempura Dipping Sauce:
1 cup water
2/3 cup soy sauce
1/3 cup mirin
1 teaspoon dashi-no-moto granules
1/2 cup finely grated daikon
1 teaspoon grated fresh ginger root

Shell and clean shrimp leaving tails on. Lightly slash under-side of shrimp diagonally. Dredge shrimp and fish with flour; set aside. To prepare Batter, combine flour with cornstarch. Beat egg with cold water; stir into flour mixture. Dip shrimp and fish into batter and fry in oil heated to 375°F until light brown. Drain on absorbent paper and serve immediately with Tempura Dipping Sauce.

To prepare the Tempura Dipping Sauce: In a saucepan, combine water, soy sauce, mirin, and dashi-no-moto; bring to a boil. Lower heat and simmer 2 to 3 minutes. Pour sauce into individual serving dishes to serve. Grated daikon and ginger may be placed in each dish. This recipe makes about 2 cups of sauce.

Variations:
• 'Ahi, aku, bass, halibut, hamachi fillet may be used.
• Vegetable tempura such as sweet potato, zucchini, pumpkin, carrot, or broccoli can be served with the seafood tempura.

2 pounds boneless chicken breasts
1/2 cup flour
2 eggs, beaten
2 cups panko or dry bread crumbs
Vegetable oil for frying

Katsu Sauce:
1/3 cup catsup
1/4 cup soy sauce
1/4 cup sugar
1-1/2 teaspoons Worcestershire sauce
Dash of pepper
2 to 3 drops hot liquid pepper sauce

Dredge chicken in flour; dip in eggs and coat with bread crumbs. Fry in oil heated to 375°F until golden brown on both sides; drain on absorbent paper. Cut into 1-inch strips and serve with Katsu Sauce.

To prepare the Katsu Sauce, stir together all ingredients. Spoon over cutlets to serve.

5 pounds beef back ribs or short ribs
1/4 cup Hawaiian (rock) salt
1 tablespoon minced garlic

Score ribs. Combine remaining ingredients; rub into meat and let stand 1 to 2 hours. Place meat on broiler rack and broil 2-inches from heat for 7 to 10 minutes. Turn and broil additional 4 to 5 minutes or until to desired doneness.

Variations:
• Fish filets: 'Ahi, Aku, Mahimahi, etc.
• Whole fish: Akule, 'Ōpakapaka, etc. Split fish before seasoning.
• Rub seasonings into filet or whole fish and let stand for 1 hour. Lightly spray broiler pan with oil. Place on cold broiler rack; broil 2 inches from heat for 2-3 minutes on each side or until desired doneness. Do not overcook.

Macadamia Crusted Mahimahi

Serves 6

2 pounds mahimahi fillet
2 cups biscuit mix
2/3 cup milk
1-1/2 cups macadamia nut bits
1/2 cup butter or margarine

Sweet Sour Sauce:
1/2 cup brown sugar, packed
1-1/2 tablespoons cornstarch
2 tablespoons soy sauce
1/2 cup white vinegar
1-1/2 cups pineapple juice

Cut mahimahi into 1-1/2-inch pieces. Stir together biscuit mix with milk; dip fish into batter then dredge with macadamia nuts. Melt butter in large skillet; pan fry fish over medium heat until golden brown. Drain on absorbent paper.

To prepare Sweet Sour Sauce, combine sugar and cornstarch in a saucepan; stir in remaining ingredients and cook over medium heat, stirring constantly, until mixture thickens. Spoon sauce over fish to serve.

4 pounds short ribs (preferably English cut)

Marinade:
3 tablespoons toasted sesame seeds
3 tablespoons sugar
3 tablespoons salad oil
1/4 cup soy sauce
1/3 cup minced onion
1/4 cup minced green onion
2 cloves garlic, minced
1/2-inch piece fresh ginger root, slivered

Cut short ribs into 2-1/2 × 2-inch pieces and score surfaces. Combine Marinade ingredients; mix well and marinate ribs 2 to 3 hours or longer. Broil 10 to 12 minutes on each side or until to desired doneness. Delicious with hot steamed rice!

1-1/2 pounds lean pork, cut in 1-inch cubes
2 teaspoons salt
1 teaspoon sherry
2 teaspoons soy sauce
1/4 cup cornstarch
3 tablespoons salad oil

Sauce:
1/2 cup brown sugar, packed
2/3 cup cider vinegar
2 tablespoons soy sauce
2 tablespoons catsup
1/2 cup pineapple syrup
4 teaspoons cornstarch

1 large tomato, wedged
1 large onion, wedged
1 medium green pepper, wedged
1 can (No. 2) pineapple chunks, drained

Combine pork, salt, sherry, soy sauce, and cornstarch; let stand 10 to 15 minutes. Heat oil and brown pork until golden; cover and simmer over medium heat 15 minutes. Drain excess fat. Stir in Sauce ingredients; bring to a boil. Add tomato, onion, green pepper, and pineapple; cook additional minute. Serve immediately.

1 pound mullet, kūmū or moi
1 teaspoon salt
1 teaspoon sugar
2 tablespoons soy sauce
3 tablespoons salad oil
1 tablespoon fresh chopped ginger root
3 tablespoons chopped green onion
Chinese parsley

Scale and clean fish. Sprinkle inside cavity and out with salt; place on shallow heat-resistant dish. Combine sugar, soy sauce, and 1 tablespoon of the oil; pour over fish. Sprinkle with ginger and green onion. Steam over boiling water for 15 minutes. Heat remaining 2 tablespoons salad oil in small pan; pour over cooked fish. Garnish with Chinese parsley and serve immediately.

1 package dried (8 ounces) or fresh (12 ounces) chow
    mein noodles
Non stick cooking spray
1/4 pound lean pork, cut in strips
1 teaspoon vegetable oil
1 clove garlic, minced
1 teaspoon sugar
1/4 teaspoon black pepper
2 tablespoons soy sauce
3 cups chicken or beef broth
1 package (12 ounces) chop suey vegetables (bean sprouts,
    carrots, watercress, onion)
3 tablespoons cornstarch
Chinese parsley (cilantro or coriander)

Cook dried noodles in boiling, unsalted water for 3 to 5
minutes. Drain and rinse with cold water; set aside. Sauté
pork in skillet coated with nonstick cooking spray; remove and
set aside. Add oil and fresh or cooked dried noodles; stir-fry 1
to 2 minutes. Place noodles on platter and keep warm. Return
pork to skillet with garlic, sugar, pepper, soy sauce, and 1 cup
broth; bring to a boil. Add vegetables and cook 1 to 2 minutes
or until crisp-tender. Mix remaining broth with cornstarch; stir
into vegetables and cook until thickened. Pour vegetables over
noodles; garnish with Chinese parsley and serve hot.

Chicken Stir-Fry

Serves 6

1/4 cup orange juice
2 teaspoons cornstarch
1 pound boneless chicken breasts, cut into strips
3/4 cup chicken broth
1-1/2 tablespoons soy sauce
2 1/2 teaspoons vegetable oil
1 clove garlic, minced
1 tablespoon minced fresh ginger root
1-1/2 cups snow peas or green peas
1 medium red bell pepper, cut into thin strips
3/4 cup sliced green onion
1 cup broccoli, sliced
1 medium carrot, thinly sliced

Combine orange juice and cornstarch in small bowl; mix well. Stir in chicken; cover and chill for 2 hours. Drain and discard marinade. In small bowl, combine broth with soy sauce; set aside.

Heat oil in large wok or nonstick skillet. Add garlic and ginger; stir-fry 30 seconds. Add chicken; stir-fry 2 to 3 minutes. Add vegetables; stir-fry until crisp-tender, about 2 to 3 minutes. Stir in broth mixture and bring to a boil. Serve immediately. Delicious with hot, steamed rice!

1 tablespoon butter or margarine
2 cups sliced chicken or beef
1 can (1 lb. 3 ounces) bamboo shoots, drained and sliced
1 can (5-3/4 ounces) button mushrooms, drained
1 can (14 ounces) shiratake, drained
1/3 cup sugar
1 cup chicken broth
1/2 cup soy sauce
1/4 cup mirin
1 block firm tofu, cubed
1 bunch watercress, cut in 1-inch lengths
1 onion, sliced
1/2 cup green onion, cut in 1-inch lengths

Melt butter in skillet; stir-fry meat. Add bamboo shoots, mushrooms, and shiratake; stir-fry for 1 minute. Add sugar, broth, soy sauce, and mirin; cook until broth comes to a boil. Add remaining ingredients and cook 1 to 2 minutes.

Variations:
• Drop a raw egg for each diner in the hot sauce; cook 1 minute.
• Add udon (noodles) in the hot sauce; cook 1 to 2 minutes.

SWEETS

1/2 cup shortening
1 cup sugar
2 eggs
1-1/4 cups flour
1 teaspoon baking soda
1/2 teaspoon salt
1 cup mashed bananas

In large mixing bowl, cream shortening and sugar. Add eggs, one at a time, beating well after each addition. Sift flour with baking soda and salt; add alternately with bananas to creamed mixture. Spoon into greased muffin pans. Bake at 350°F for 15 to 20 minutes or until toothpick inserted in center comes out clean.

Tip: Quick breads like muffins and biscuits are so called because they are quickly mixed and need no lengthy rising time before baking because they do not use yeast as an ingredient.

1 egg, slightly beaten
1 cup milk
1/2 teaspoon lemon extract
2 cups biscuit mix
4 slices bread
1 quart oil for frying
1/2 cup sugar

Combine egg, milk, and lemon extract; add to biscuit mix all at once. Mix batter until smooth.

Cut each slice of bread into 9 squares and coat with batter. Drop each batter-coated piece of bread into oil heated to 375°F and cook about 2 minutes or until golden brown on both sides. Drain on absorbent paper; roll in sugar before serving.

Papaya-Pineapple Jam

Makes 4 (6-ounce) jars

3 cups chopped papaya
2 cups chopped pineapple
1/3 cup lemon juice
1/4 cup orange juice
1 teaspoon fresh ginger juice
Grate rind of 1 lemon
Grated rind of 1/2 orange
Sugar

Combine fruits, juices, and rinds in a saucepan. Cook 30 minutes, stirring occasionally. Measure cooked fruit mixture; combine with equal amount of sugar. Cook over low heat about 30 minutes or until mixture thickens, stirring frequently to prevent burning. Pour jam into hot, sterilized jars and seal with melted paraffin while the jam is hot. Delicious on toast! Also makes a delicious glaze for baked ham and pork chops.

Tips:
• Sirupy jelly may be caused by too much sugar, undercooking, or too long cooking of very acetic juice and sugar.
• Tough or rubbery jelly may be the result of too little sugar or overcooking.
• Very dark jelly may be the result of too slow cooking or cooking in too large quantities.

6 firm-ripe bananas
1 tablespoon lemon juice
1/2 cup bread crumbs
1/3 cup brown sugar, packed
1/2 teaspoon ground cinnamon
1/4 cup butter or margarine

Ice cream, optional

Grease 2-quart baking dish; set aside. Peel and cut bananas into 1/2-inch slices; place into prepared baking dish; sprinkle with lemon juice and toss. Combine bread crumbs, brown sugar, and cinnamon; cut in butter then sprinkle over bananas. Bake at 350°F for 30 minutes or until golden brown. If desired, serve with ice cream.

Tips:
• Cinnamon is made from rolled, pressed and dried tree bark, usually cassia (*Cinnamomum cassia*). It has a sweet flavor in both stick and ground form.
• Most manufacturers and merchants agree that whole and ground spices have a two-year shelf life once opened. Best stored away from heat.

1 box (18.5 ounces) chocolate cake mix
1/3 cup sugar
1/3 cup cornstarch
3/4 cup water
1 can (12 ounces) frozen coconut milk, thawed
2 cups sweetened whipped cream
Chocolate curls or freshly grated coconut

Prepare and bake cake in 9 × 13 × 2-inch pan according to
package directions. Cool and split cake into two thin layers.

To prepared haupia, combine sugar, cornstarch, water, and
coconut milk in saucepan while stirring constantly to prevent
lumping. Cook over low heat, stirring constantly, until mixture
thickens. Remove from heat and cool to room temperature.
Spread cooled haupia between layers and on top of cake; let
stand until firm. Refrigerate to chill well.

Top cake with sweetened whipped cream and garnish with
chocolate curls or grated coconut to serve.

Tropical Nut Bread

Makes 1 loaf

2 cups flour
2 teaspoons baking powder
1 teaspoon baking soda
1/2 teaspoon salt
1 can (8-1/4 ounces) crushed pineapple, including liquid
1 cup mashed ripe bananas
1/3 cup orange juice
1/2 cup butter or margarine
1 cup sugar
2 eggs
1 cup macadamia nut bits

Sift flour with baking powder, baking soda, and salt. Combine pineapple, including liquid, bananas, and orange juice. In large bowl, cream butter and sugar until light and fluffy; add eggs, one at a time, beating well after each addition. Add flour alternately with pineapple mixture, mixing only enough to moisten flour. Stir in nuts. Pour into a greased 9 × 5 × 3-inch loaf pan. Bake at 350°F for 1 hour and 15 minutes, or until done.

3 1/2 cups puffed rice cereal
1 cup quick-cooking oats
3/4 cup toasted sesame seeds
1 package (10 ounces) marshmallows
1/2 cup peanut butter
1/4 cup butter or margarine
1/4 cup macadamia nut bits
1/2 cup raisins

Grease 9 × 13 × 2-inch pan. In saucepan, combine rice cereal, oats, and sesame seeds; toast over medium heat for 1 to 2 minutes. In large saucepan, combine and melt marshmallows, peanut butter, and butter over low heat. Stir in cereal mixture, macadamia nuts, and raisins. Pour mixture into prepared pan; press down firmly and let cool. Cut into bars and wrap individually with waxed paper; store in airtight jar.

4 envelopes unflavored gelatin
3 cups hot water
3 tablespoons instant Kona coffee granules
2 tablespoons sugar
1 can (14 ounces) sweetened condensed milk

Dissolve gelatin in hot water. Stir in coffee and sugar. Add condensed milk and stir well to combine; pour into 8-inch square pan. Chill until set. Cut into serving pieces.

1/2 cup butter or margarine
1/2 cup brown sugar, packed
1 egg, slightly beaten
1 egg yolk, slightly beaten
1/4 teaspoon vanilla extract
1-1/2 cups flour
1/4 teaspoon baking soda
1/4 teaspoon salt
1 can (6 ounces) pecan halves, split
1 egg white

Chocolate Frosting:
2 squares (1 ounce each) unsweetened chocolate
1/4 cup milk
1 tablespoon butter
1 cup powdered sugar

Cream butter and sugar until light and fluffy; beat in egg, egg yolk, and vanilla. Sift together flour, baking soda, and salt; add gradually to creamed butter mixture; mix well.

Arrange pecans into groups of five on greased baking sheet to resemble "head" and "legs" of turtle. Form rounded teaspoonfuls of dough into balls; dip bottoms into egg white and press lightly onto nuts. Bake at 350°F for 10 minutes. Cool and frost tops with Chocolate Frosting.

To prepare Chocolate Frosting, combine chocolate, milk, and butter in bowl or small saucepan; heat in microwave oven or over surface burner set low until chocolate melts. Remove from heat and add powdered sugar; beat until smooth. Add more milk if needed to obtain right consistency to frost cookies.

Tips:
• Chocolate will keep for a year at room temperature. It is best to keep it stored below 70 degrees Fahrenheit.
• Chocolate can sometimes be a little finicky, so for best results, store it in a cool, dry place, chop it even, and melt it gently.

3 tablespoons cornstarch
3/4 cup sugar
1/4 teaspoon salt
1/2 cup macadamia nut bits
4 eggs, separated
2 cups milk, scalded
1 tablespoon butter
1 teaspoon vanilla

9-inch baked pie shell
Sweetened whipped cream
1/4 cup macadamia nut bits

Combine cornstarch, 1/2 cup sugar, salt, and macadamia nuts; add egg yolks, stirring until well blended. Stir in milk slowly and blend thoroughly. Cook over medium heat, stirring constantly, until mixture thickens. Add butter and vanilla. Cool 1 hour.

In medium bowl, beat egg whites until soft peaks form. Gradually add remaining 1/4 cup sugar, beating until stiff; fold into cooled custard mixture. Pour into baked pie shell; refrigerate and chill until set, about 2 to 3 hours. Garnish with sweetened whipped cream and remaining macadamia nuts.

Variations:
• **Coconut Cream Pie:** Substitute grated coconut for macadamia nut bits.
• **Banana Cream Pie:** Omit macadamia nuts and place banana slices between layers in cream custard filling.

2 envelopes unflavored gelatin
3-2/3 cups water
1/3 cup sweetened condensed milk
2-1/2 teaspoons almond extract
1 can Mandarin oranges, drained
1 can (20 ounces) lychees, drained, optional

Dissolve gelatin in water and bring to a boil, stirring until gelatin is completely dissolved. Gradually stir in condensed milk and almond extract; mix well and pour into 8 × 8-inch pan; refrigerate until firm, about 3 to 4 hours. Cut into cubes or desired sizes and serve in bowls garnished with Mandarin oranges or lychees.

Variations:
• Canned fruit cocktail may be substituted for Mandarin oranges and lychee.
• Canned pineapple chunks may be served with Almond Tofu.

1 envelope unflavored gelatin
1/4 cup water
4 eggs, separated
1/4 cup lemon juice
2 tablespoons sugar
1 can (6 ounces) frozen guava juice, thawed
Few drops red food coloring
1/4 teaspoon salt
1/2 cup sugar
9-inch baked pie shell
Sweetened whipped cream

Sprinkle gelatin over water to soften. Beat egg yolks well. In a saucepan, combine egg yolks, lemon juice, and the 2 tablespoons sugar; cook over low heat, stirring constantly, until mixture thickens. Stir in softened gelatin and remove from heat; cool slightly, then stir in guava juice and few drops food coloring until mixture is pink. Chill until mixture begins to thicken. In small mixer bowl, beat egg whites with salt until soft peaks form. Beat in remaining 1/2 cup sugar until stiff peaks form; fold in chilled guava mixture. Pour into pie shell; refrigerate until firm, about 1 to 2 hours. Garnish with sweetened whipped cream to serve.

1 package (10 ounces) mochiko (rice flour)
3/4 cup brown sugar, packed
2 cups shredded coconut
1 cup coconut milk
1 quart canola or vegetable oil for frying

Mix dry ingredients together; add coconut milk and stir only
enough to moisten dry ingredients. Form into 1-inch balls or
drop by teaspoonfuls into oil heated to 375°F. Fry until golden
brown on all sides. Drain on absorbent paper and serve hot
or cold.

DRINKS

Mai Tai

Serves 1

Mai Tai means "good" or "out of this world" and
following is one version of it.

1/2 lime
1 ounce lemon juice
1 ounce Mai Tai Mix*
1-1/4 ounces amber (St. James) rum
1-1/4 ounces Lemon Hart 86 proof rum

Garnishes:
Mint
Pineapple spear
Maraschino cherry
Sugar cane stick
Vanda or dendrobium orchid

Squeeze 1/2 lime and leave shell in glass. Fill glass with
shaved ice. Blend remaining ingredients. Serve in 13-ounce
doubled old-fashioned glass. Garnish with sprig of fresh
mint, spear of fresh pineapple, maraschino cherry stick of
sugar cane and float an orchid.

Note: *Mai Tai Mix: 1/3 ounce orgeat syrup, 1/3 ounce rock
candy syrup and 1/3 ounce orange curacao.

Banana Milk Shake

Serves 2

2 cups milk
1 ripe banana, sliced
2 tablespoons pineapple juice
2 tablespoons sugar, optional
1/2 teaspoon vanilla, optional

Combine all ingredients in a blender; blend until smooth or to desired consistency.

Passion Fruit Punch

Serves 6

2 cups passion fruit juice
1/2 cup orange juice
1/3 cup lime juice
1 cup freshly brewed tea
1/2 cup sugar
2 cups ginger ale

Combine all ingredients and stir until sugar dissolves.
Refrigerate to chill and serve over ice cubes or crushed ice.

Hawaiian Lemonade

Serves 6

1 can (6 ounces) frozen lemonade, thawed
1 can (6 ounces) frozen pineapple juice, thawed
1 bottle (28 ounces) sparkling water, chilled

Combine undiluted fruit juices; add chilled sparkling water just before serving. Serve over ice; garnish with mint leaves, if desired.

Mango Nectar

1/3 cup sugar
3 cups water
1/3 cup lemon juice
1-1/4 cups mango pulp
1 cup fresh orange juice

Combine sugar and water; stir until sugar dissolves. Stir in
remaining ingredients; refrigerate until chilled and serve over
crushed ice.

Frosted Hawaiian Coffee

Serves 4–5

2 cups strong chilled Kona coffee
1 cup chilled pineapple juice
1 pint coffee or vanilla ice cream, softened

Combine all ingredients; beat until smooth and frothy. Pour into tall glasses to serve. If desired, may be topped with whipped cream.

Glossary

A

'Ahi: Hawaiian name for yellowfin tuna

Aku: Hawaiian name for skipjack tuna

Akule: Mackerel

Almond tofu: Chinese gelatin dessert with fruit

C

Cascaron: Filipino-style fried coconut doughnuts

Char siu: Chinese sweet roasted pork

Char siu bao: Chinese pork-filled bun

Chinese parsley: Cilantro, coriander

Chop suey vegetables: Combination of bean sprouts, carrots, watercress, green onion

Chutney: Spicy relish made with fruits, spices, and herbs

Coconut milk: Juice from the meat of coconut

D

Daikon: Japanese name for large white radish

Dashi-no-moto: Soup stock base or granules

G

Ginger: A brown, fibrous rhizome whose root is used for flavoring

H

Hamachi: Japanese name for yellowtail tuna

Haupia: Hawaiian coconut pudding

Hawaiian salt: Coarse, rock salt

Honu: Hawaiian word for turtle

K

Kalbi kui: Korean barbecued short ribs

Kim chee: Korean hot, spicy, preserved vegetable, usually cabbage

Kona: Region on the island of Hawai'i

Kūmū: Hawaiian name for goatfish

L

Liliko'i: Hawaiian word for passion fruit

Lychee: Round, sweet, juicy, white fruit covered with a rough, red skin

M

Macadamia nut: A rich, oily nut grown in Hawai'i

Mahimahi: Hawaiian for dolphinfish

Malasadas: Portuguese hole-less doughnuts, deep-fried and rolled in sugar

Mango: A gold and green tropical fruit

Mirin: Japanese sweet rice wine

Mochiko: Japanese name for glutinous rice flour

Moi: Hawaiian name for threadfish

N

Nam Pla: Asian fish sauce

Nigiri sushi: Japanese vinegar-flavored rice pressed into thumb-shape topped with seafood

O

'Ōpakapaka: Hawaiian name for blue snapper

P

Panko: Japanese flour meal for breading

Passion fruit: A tangy, plum-sized tropical fruit; also called liliko'i

Poke: Hawaiian seafood appetizer

Pūlehu: Hawaiian method of barbecuing; or broiling

Pūpū: Hawaiian name for appetizer or hors d'oeuvres

S

Shiratake: Japanese gelatinous noodle-like strips made from tuberous root flour

Soy sauce: Favorite Japanese seasoning sauce made from fermented soybeans

Sukiyaki: Japanese meat/chicken and vegetable dish

Sushi: Japanese vinegared rice

T

Tempura: Japanese fritters

Teriyaki: Japanese soy-flavored sauce

Tofu: Japanese name for soybean curd

Torikatsu: Japanese chicken cutlet

W

Wasabi: Japanese name for horse-radish

Won ton chips: Fried thin strips of dough used to make won ton